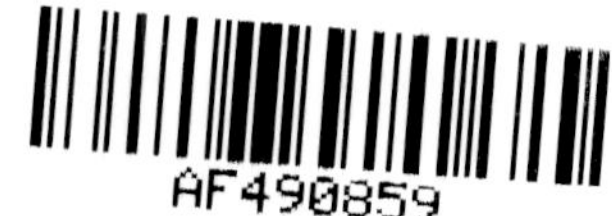

This Notebook belongs to :

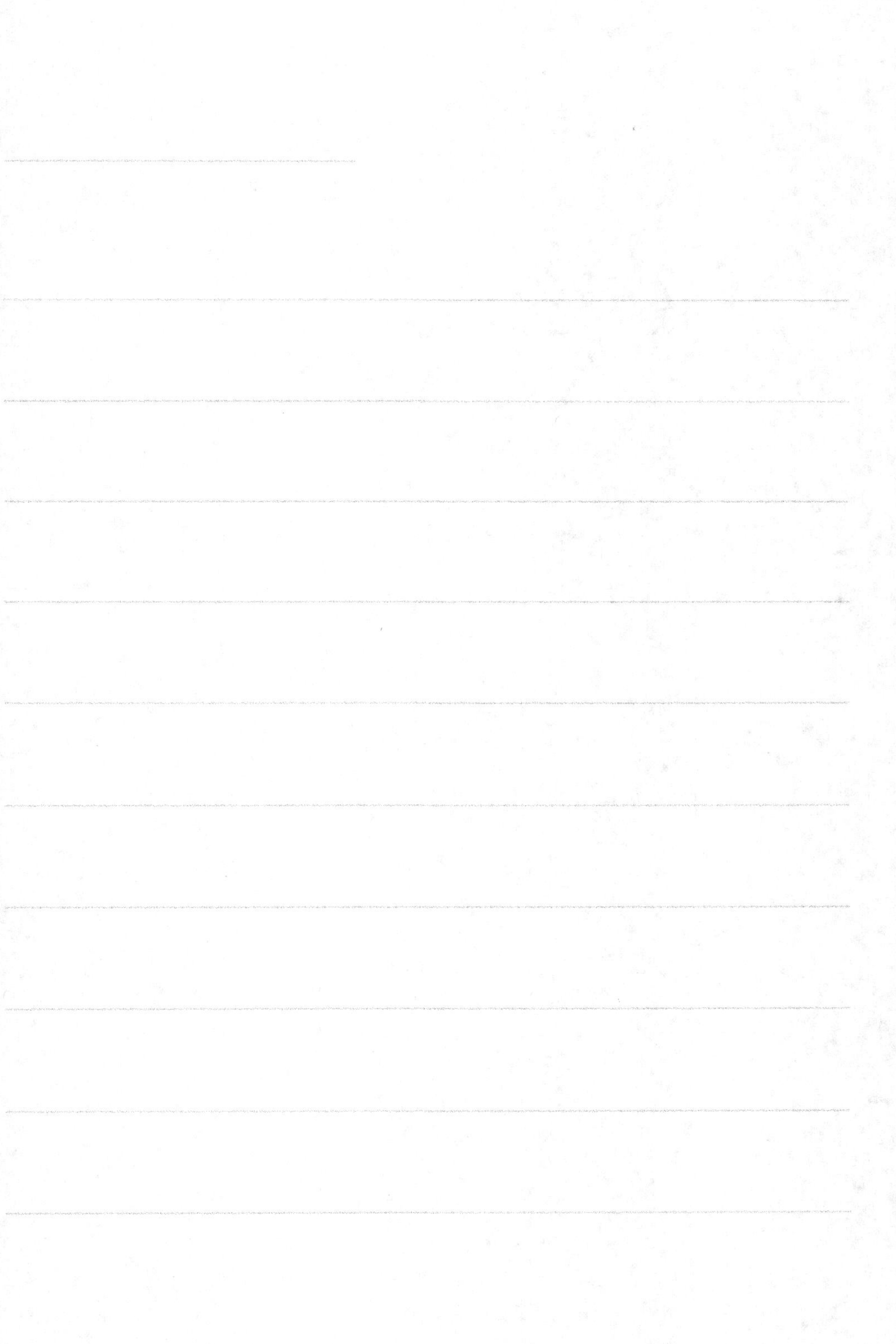

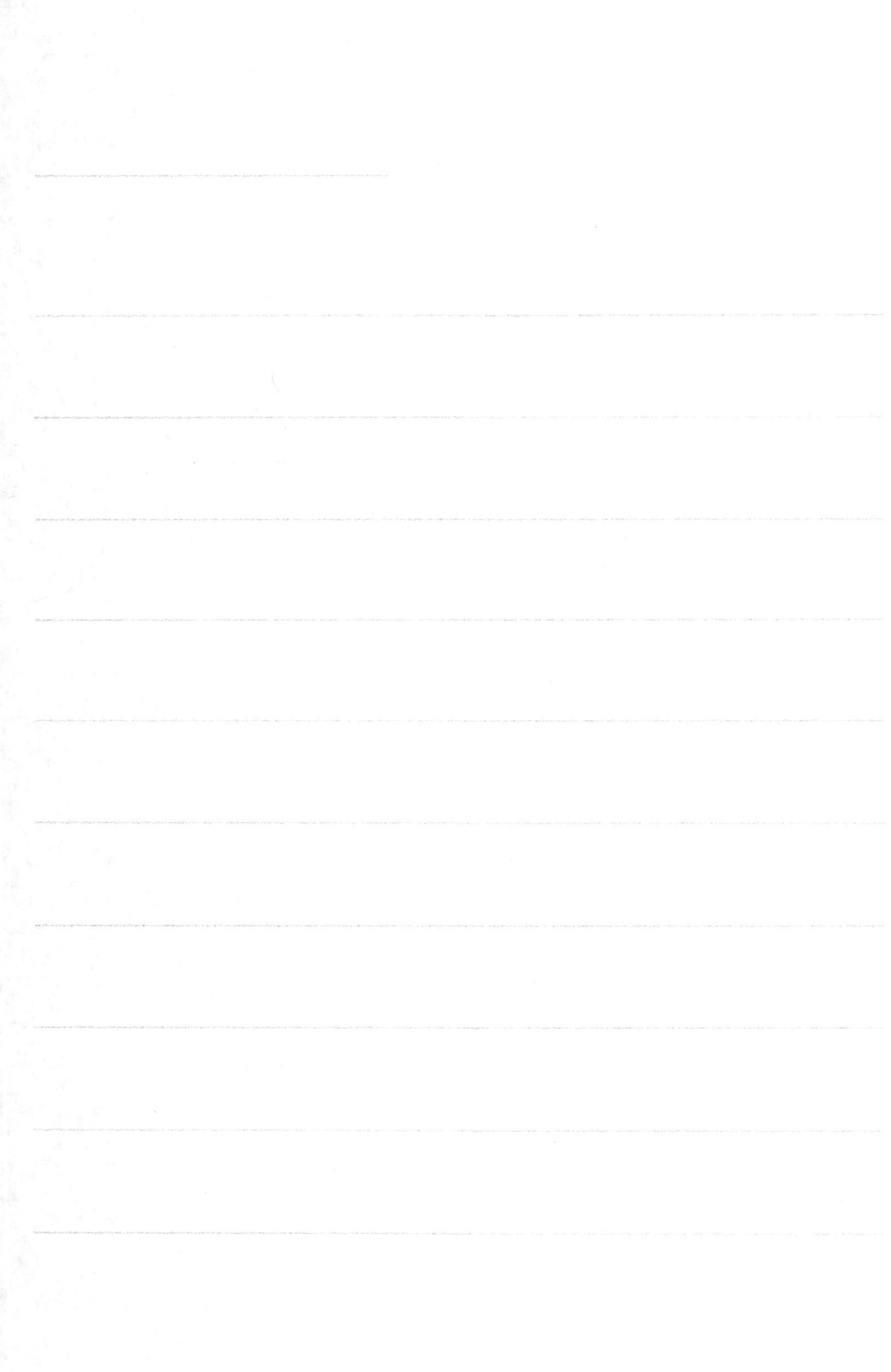

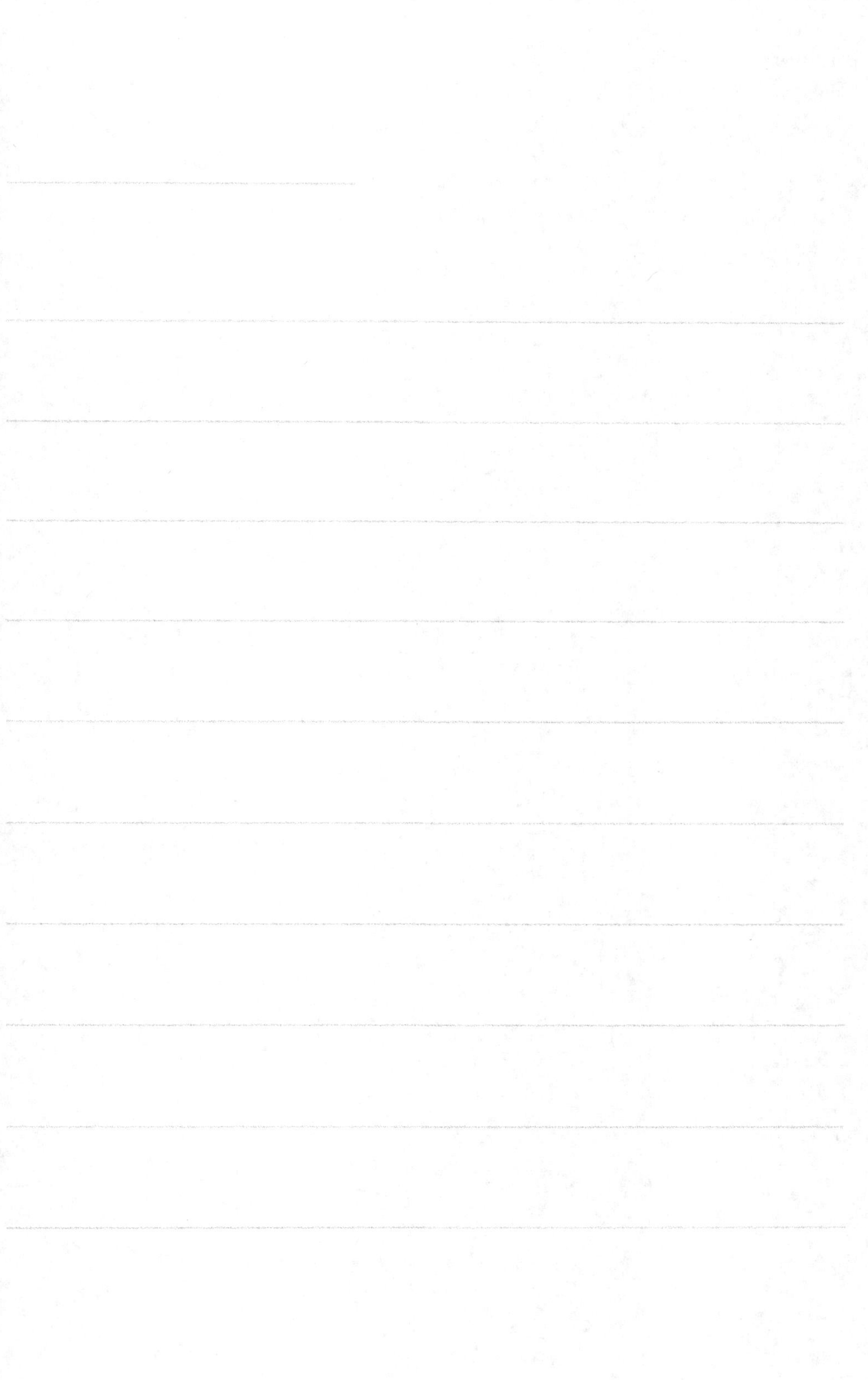

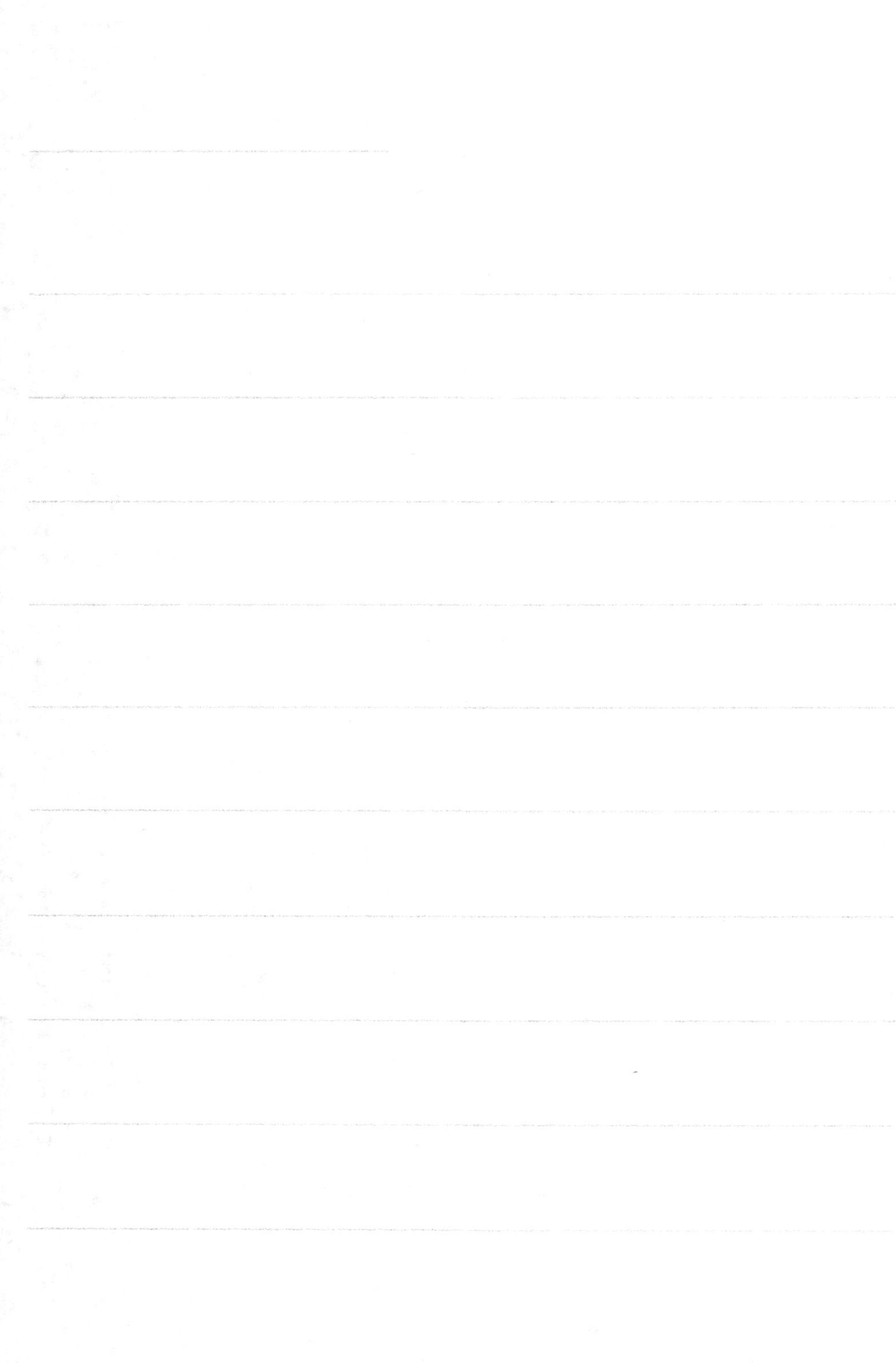